THE COMPLETE BEGINNER'S GUIDE TO BEEKEEPING

Copyright © 2018 Mark B. Chase

All Rights Reserved. No portion of this book may be reproduced or used in any manner whatsoever without the expressed written permission of the author.

TABLE OF CONTENTS

Introduction 1

    A brief history 6

Chapter One: About the Bees 9

    What Does a Honey Bee Looks Like?................. 11

    Anatomy of a honey bee.....................................12

    Behavior of the honey bee.................................14

    Honey bee distribution 16

    Pollination 18

    Honey Bee Dance... 20

Chapter Two: Responsibilities of Each Bee 23

    Queen Bee.. 25

    Drones 27

Workers 29

Other Important information you need to know 31

Chapter Three: Getting Started With Beekeeping 34

Learn about beekeeping 36

Setting up Your Hive 41

Placing Your Hives in the Optimal Location 47

Placing the Bees in the Hive 50

Tending to Your Bees 56

Chapter Four: About Beekeeping 62

Beekeeping Equipment 62

Spring Feeding your Bees 69

Smoking bees 75

Bee Swarming 79

Harvesting Honey 85

Conclusion 87

INTRODUCTION

Thank you for choosing this book. This comprehensive guide will enlighten you on everything you need to know to start keeping bees in your backyard, from purchasing honey bees and setting up your hive to collecting honey and averting bee swarming.

Imagine inhaling the sweet scent that emanates from fruit blossom and other vegetation. Then, you ought to seriously think about obtaining a colony. Anyone can be successful with bees even in the arid North and Southwest into Canada, almost every part of the world except in the glacial regions, where it is difficult to raise anything effectively.

Do not allow the fear of the little creatures prevent you from doing this easy, lucrative and fascinating project. It is true that modern bees that are kept by beekeepers do sting, but that happens very rarely, only when you might have made a wrong move (not because they don't like you or that they are nasty).

Typically, these insects do not even realize that you are there since they're one creature humans have not succeeded in taming. The colony you see in a backyard is just as wild as the swarm you will find in the forest. However, the difference lies in your attitude as well as some essential equipment. When you have a smoker, bee veil, and maybe bee gloves, you can easily turn the apparently rowdy mound of pulsating life into docile little creatures you can handle easily.

As a reward for your care, the little golden critters will produce several pounds of honey for your use at home, sale or gifts. The excess beeswax will be really useful for some fine candles with a natural and sweet perfume as well as a dazzling flame. After sometimes, when you have enough colonies, you may sell your wax so that it can be recycled back to the bees as a form of foundation for comb-building.

Honey bees are also good at pollinating crops. They have been the major pollinators of flowers for millions of years and for that reason, the plants that produce the flowers have relied on the honey bees

Yes, you can still get started with your bees adventure this spring and get more than enough honey than you can use by the end of summer; however, you should get started now. This is due to the fact that the first honey flow occurs around June, and you need a very healthy colony that contains lots of babies called brood and even more adult bees, that are ready to start foraging for pollen and nectar. When you start out weak in early summer, you'll be able to save just a little excess honey, and you may end up saving all of it to feed your bees during the next winter. So, act fast now if you want any of the honey harvests for yourself.

Thank you again for purchasing this book. I hope you enjoy it!

A BRIEF HISTORY

Humans have been involved with honey bees for thousands of years. In Spain, there are cave paintings of men that were harvesting honey from trees (dated to fifteen thousand years ago). Some Egyptian tombs pictograms show beekeeping management about 4,500 years ago. Up to the middle of the 19th century, beekeepers use containers made of clay to keep their bees. Bees were mostly obtained naturally by a swarm or by gathering a calm swarm of bushes. By the end of a season, honey and wax were taken from the bees by means of destroying most, if not all of the combs created by those little critters.

The ability of these wonderful creatures to withstand the harsh treatment meted to them by humans has been amazing and they have been able to acclimatize to the harsh environments of the world, existing in areas where humans live, from the equator to beyond the Arctic Circle. Most domesticated bees descended from a little number of queen bees from their first countries, which are Africa and Europe. Honey bees have survived via natural selection methods in those regions.

If these little creatures were to disappear from this planet, humans would have just four years until a severe shortage of food would start. Honey bees perform numerous pollination services; just think about the legumes, vegetables, seeds, nuts, and fruits we consume. Majority of these food items were pollinated by honey bees.

By the middle of the 19th century, some discoveries help to drastically change the methods of keeping bees eternally. A simple discovery indicates that if there is a bee space of between 6mm to 9mm left, the little creatures won't seal it up with propolis (a gum-like substance) or even try to make use of the space by creating a comb across it. Thus, this finding resulted in the creation and designing of hives which allow the housing and movement of combs for inspection and this is the foundation of all recent hive design.

CHAPTER ONE: ABOUT THE BEES

Honey bees are popular but they represent only a little percentage of the bee species. They are the only surviving group from the Apini tribe, under the Apis genus. Honey bees are well known for secreting and storing honey and constructing remarkably huge nests with the wax produced by worker bees in a colony. Honey bees are members of the insect class, which is called Insecta. The insects are members of the subfamily Apinae, which create and store honey.

Honey bees are social critters that procure a caste structure for the accomplishment of tasks that guarantee the continued existence of the colony. Several thousands of bee workers which are all sterile females take charge of nursing, cleaning, feeding and defending the group. On the other hand, the male drones are responsible for mating the queen, who is the only fertile female in a colony.

WHAT DOES A HONEY BEE LOOKS LIKE?

A honey bee has a light brown color and measures about 15 mm long. It is an oval-shaped creature with a brown band and golden-yellow color. Though honey bees' body color differs between species and some of them have mainly black bodies, nearly all honey bees possess varying light-to-dark striations. The dark and light stripes help with the survival of the honey bees; the brightly colored body of a honey bee serves as a warning to honey robbers or predators of the honey bee's capacity to sting. This is unlike other bee species that hide upon sensing predators close by.

ANATOMY OF A HONEY BEE

The body of a honey bee is divided into; 6 visible segments of the abdomen, 3 segments of thorax, antennae, legs, and stinger.

The honey bee's head consists of feeding structures, antennae and eyes. The eyes comprise the simple eye and the compound eye: the simple eye (ocelli) helps the bee to determine the amount of light present, while the compound eye enables the bee to recognize light, color and directional information from the UV rays of the sun. The bee's antenna helps to measure flight speed and to smell and sense odors. The bee's jaw, which is the mandible is used to eat pollen, cut and shape wax, feed the queen and larvae, clean the hive as well as for grooming and fighting.

The bee's thorax includes legs, wings and the muscles that control movements. The forewing is typically larger than the hind wing and it is used as a cooling mechanism and also for flight, while the hindwing is used to cool the hive by fanning away heat. The six segments of the abdomen consist of a stinger in the workers and queen, female reproductive organs in the queen and male reproductive organs in the drone.

BEHAVIOR OF THE HONEY BEE

The honey bee hives are generally found in rock crevices and in the holes of trees in the wild. The worker bees create hive from the wax secreted from their special abdominal glands. They also gather some flakes of wax produced from their abdomens and masticate the flakes until soft. These workers then shape the wax and use it to make cells to create the hive. Honey bees, unlike other species of bees, do not hibernate during the cold months. They only stay inside their nests, huddle closely together, share body heat and feed on stored foods.

Honey bees are social critters that live in colonies. Nonetheless, these little creatures display hostile behaviors in their colonies; a queen will sting other queens in the mating fights for supremacy, and the drones get ejected from their nests during the cold period. Honey bees play an important role in ecology and pollination, yet measures should be taken when handling them. Make sure you contact a pest control professional before you attempt to address a swarm.

HONEY BEE DISTRIBUTION

Honey bees species can be found worldwide and are seen in many places, including the United States and Europe. These species are most noticeable in late spring and summer when the new queens relocate from their old colonies to build new nests with thousands of worker bees. During this period, you will see large groups of bees swarming together to find a new nesting site and it takes a swarm of bee about 24 hours to discover a new nesting place. Although most swarms of bees are harmless, some species are exceptionally hostile and might attack unprovoked.

Since honey bees can be found all over the world, their behavior and nature may vary. For example, German and African honey bees are known to display remarkable defensive behavior while Italian honey bees are often more domesticated. Nevertheless, all honey bees can be extremely defensive when provoked and they are capable of chasing animals or humans hundreds of feet.

POLLINATION

Honey bees have been the major pollinators of flowers for millions of years and for that reason, the plants that produce the flowers have relied on the honey bees. Reproduction is the goal of the plant and the honey bees help to accomplish this goal by innocently transferring pollen (plant's male sperm cells) from one flower to another. Therefore, in the absence of pollination, most plant won't be able to reproduce and would die out eventually.

Human beings derive benefits from this relationship through honey production and crop harvest. Most of the crops we eat were pollinated by the bees. And this is the major reason many farmers maintain honey bee colonies because plants won't produce vegetables and fruits without pollination. Apart from pollination, honey bees take out nectar along with pollen from the flowers. They transport the nectar to their nests and convert it into honey through a process.

HONEY BEE DANCE

Two major theories are available on the way honey bee workers communicate with one another about a new source of food; the odor plume and the dance. Though there are proves to support each assertion, the honey bee dance is generally more accepted. The honey bee dance language includes dancing and odor as a means of communication, yet the odor plume theory suggests that the bee enlistment solely depends on floral odor. The dance performs a significant role in the survival of the honey bee's species; it has remained one of the significant techniques used in food foraging.

Honey bees use the dance to communicate with one another especially when a new food source has been discovered. If a worker finds out an abundant food source; when she returns to the nest, she'll dance in a circle to notify the others of her findings.

There are two types of honey bee dances; waggle dance and round dance. The waggle dance is when a bee waggles its abdomen like figure 8 pattern and this indicates that the food source is more than 150 meters. While the round dance is a movement in a circle which indicates that the food source distance is less than 50 meters from their nest. The accurate distance is communicated with the dance duration.

The dance language is understood by some humans. Researchers can verify the efficacy by measuring the quality and quantity of new nectar and pollen brought into the nest by the bee. Although, some characteristics of the dance language are still not known, especially the facts that these little creatures understand the entire dance patterns even in the dark.

CHAPTER TWO: RESPONSIBILITIES OF EACH BEE

Honey bees, like other bee species, are social creatures that live in colonies numbering in the thousands. There are three types of adult honey bees that reside in a colony; the queen, drones, and workers.

QUEEN BEE

The queen is the principal adult female bee and the mother of most or all of the bees in the hive. The worker bees choose a future queen bee's larva and it's nourished with royal jelly, which is a protein-rich secretion. This enables the queen bee's larva to be sexually mature.

The newly hatched queen bee will start her life in a duel to the death with any other queens she can find in the colony as well as destroy potential rivals that are yet to be hatched. When she completes this task, she embarks on her virgin mating flight. A queen bee lays eggs and produces a pheromone that helps to keep all the females in the colony sterile throughout her life. Each colony has only one queen bee, which has the ability to lay two thousand eggs a day.

DRONES

The drones are the male bees that are the products of unfertilized eggs. A drone has bigger eyes and does not have a stinger. These creatures do not have the parts of the body for the collection of nectar or pollen, so they can't help in feeding the community either can they defend the hive.

The only job of the drone is to mate with the queen. Mating happens in flight, which is why the drones have large eyes for better vision.

When a drone succeeds in mating, it dies soon because its penis and related abdominal tissues get ripped out of its body after mating. At the period of colder winters, the worker bees protect the food stores and stop the drones from entering the hive because they're no longer needed, making them starve to death.

WORKERS

The worker bees are females and they are responsible for doing all chores except reproduction, which is the sole responsibility of the queen bee. The worker bees tend to their queen in their first days and remain busy for the rest of their short lives.

The workers perform many roles which include guarding the hive against attackers like wasps, fanning the hive to maintain the right temperature, carrying water, foraging for food and nectar, removing the dead, storing pollen, building honeycomb, feeding drones, and preserving honey.

Workers can also make the decision to move the colony in a swarm and then build a new nest.

To maintain a right temperature for the hive is essential for the continued existence of the eggs and larvae. The chamber for the young must be at a stable temperature for the incubation of the eggs. If the temperature gets too hot, the worker bees gather water and drop it around the hive, and then start fanning the air with their wings to bring about cooling by evaporation. On the other hand, if it gets too cold, the workers come together to generate body heat.

OTHER IMPORTANT INFORMATION YOU NEED TO KNOW

The queen bee in a hive spends all or most of her time in the brood chamber. She is groomed and fed by young workers; in turn, she lays up to 3,000 eggs daily. Recent research has found that the presence of the queen bee in a colony is very important because she secretes an unidentified "queen substance" which helps to keep the colony in a healthy, productive state and prevent the workers from laying eggs. Some of the workers can lay eggs in the absence of a queen; however, such eggs can only produce drones (non-working males). This will make the colony become weak and dispirited.

Without the queen's secretion, the bees get to know about this within minutes that they don't have a queen and this makes them loud, nasty and worked up. But you shouldn't worry about this since you'll be purchasing a healthy young queen with your colony and she'll live for about 2 to 5 years.

Since it is not advisable to keep the queen in the upper storage sections of a hive to lay her eggs, you may top the brood chamber with a device known as "queen excluder"; it's a flat frame that is the same length and width as the hive's other sections. It's covered with a heavy inset wire screen and the openings in the mesh enable the workers to pass through and drop excess honey in the upper stories but the opening is not big enough for the queen.

However, some experts have frowned at the use of queen excluder since it can result in swarming and possible loss of about half of the colony. Therefore, another option is to keep providing the queen with empty comb in the brood chamber; this will make her stay and lay eggs there.

It is also important to note that honey should not be taken from the brood chamber where the queen is raising the young bees. You need to leave that part of the hive strictly alone while you check once or twice a week to check for signs of disease and to see how laying is progressing. You can also divide the colony artificially before swarming time, though you can only harvest honey from a hive's supers.

CHAPTER THREE: GETTING STARTED WITH BEEKEEPING

Keeping bees is like engaging in any other form of livestock management, a bee colony requires good shelter to be sound, well fed and disease free. A good beekeeper needs to understand the sound of bees, their behaviors, and their daily needs.

Honey bees are wonderful creatures that produce the honey we use as well as performing many other useful tasks like pollinating crops, for human beings. When keeping bees, you are helping their colonies to thrive and you also gain from them by collecting honey in return. Starting a beekeeping project is very easy and it can be a cool project for you to do in your backyard. All you need to do is get enlightened with bees, how to take care of them and the supplies required to keep them thriving and healthy.

LEARN ABOUT BEEKEEPING

1. Before you start a beekeeping project, it is essential that you get to know more about them. You can take a beekeeping course. There are many colleges and universities that offer beekeeping classes for community education programs. Check out the ones in your state or region. Moreover, some beekeeping organizations host introductory classes for people who will like to start beekeeping projects. Therefore, perform an online research on classes for beekeeping in your area. Similarly, most schools of agriculture offer such a course. Although such class may be expensive, you'll learn many things you need to know about keeping bees.

2. Furthermore, try to learn some things from a beekeeper. Someone who is already into beekeeping will be able to give you one or two tips about caring for bees. This is especially important if you're planning to become a professional beekeeper. Typically, an experienced beekeeper will be able to answer any question you ask and should give you some useful advice you need to start up your own colony. You may consider offering to help a beekeeper with beekeeping for free in exchange for beekeeping information and advice. Some hands-on beekeeping experience before starting your own can be very useful, including the fact that the beekeeper will most likely appreciate the free labor you provided.

3. In many cases, the best approach to begin keeping bees is to join a nearby beekeeping association that has a beginner's courses and possibly has a preparation apiary where one can get some experience and learn from local beekeepers prior to starting your own project. In most cases, the only expense you may expend is for joining such Association because they'll have bees and skilled beekeepers that will show and guide prospective beekeepers on managing a colony as well as bee equipment to loan for the training. It is, however, advisable to go through a season in the training apiary before you spend lots of money to set up your own. It is even possible that the association

sells new or fairly used bee equipment that you can purchase to start your own craft.

4. Make sure to start out with just a few hives. You may decide to become a beekeeper with just a hive or many, many hives. The amount you decide to tend to largely depends on how dedicated you are and what you want to get out of your efforts. However, if you are just beginning a beekeeping project, it is advisable to start small to figure out how you'll take care of your bees before you invest a lot of efforts and time in many hives. For somebody who just wants to obtain some honey for his/her family and wants his/her garden to be pollinated, one or two hives may be enough to achieve this. But for someone who wants to get enough honey for

sale, many more hives may be required to produce enough honey to sell. Generally, a well-established hive may generate about 11 kg (25 pounds) of honey

SETTING UP YOUR HIVE

1. The first thing to do in this step is to buy a hive. You may acquire a "starter kit" that will include all the components of the hive that is required for starting beekeeping project. This kit can be gotten from some farm supply stores and also online. It consists of the essential equipment needed to get going with beekeeping. Although the exact components of the kit vary, it should have:

- Hive Boxes (2 or 3)

- Bee feeder

- Hive stand

- Hive Inner Cover

- Hive Outer Cover

- Bottom Board

- Frames

2. Purchase the tools you'll need to take care of your bees. After setting up a hive and placing the bees in it, there are some tools you'll need to handle them. These tools include;

- A smoker with a shield to make the bees docile whenever you want to go into the hive

- A mini crowbar which is used to take the hive apart

- A bee brush for moving bees around when you're dealing with the frames. The bee brush will enable you to remove the bees from the frames without hurting them.

- An extractor which is especially useful for harvesting a lot of honey. An extractor is a machine that you can place the honeycomb frames in it and it extracts honey from the comb with centrifugal force

3. Buy protective clothing. A beekeeping project requires purchasing the right clothing to protect you from getting stung by bees. As you get used to handling the bees you may not need all the protection anymore but it is important to start out with protection to ensure that you're safe around

these little creatures. Some of the protective clothing you may need to acquire includes:

- Bee suit
- Gloves
- Hard hat made to be used with a veil
- Round tie-down veil

4. Choose a good location for your hive. A hive should be set up in a place with little human traffic and with nearby flowers. Make sure you pick a location that's relatively protected from high winds. If you have a garden, place your hive nearby but ensure it is placed behind a small fence or barrier to prevent the bees from flying directly over your

garden paths. The small fence or barrier will force the bees to fly up and over your garden path on their way to the garden beds. Keep in mind that the type of flowers that is near your hive will affect the flavor of the honey that your bees will produce. Generally, hives can be positioned in backyards, even with close by neighbors without problems. Your neighbors may not even notice them, but it is advisable to inform your neighbors prior to setting up the hive to ensure none of them are allergic to bees. It is possible for local, country and/or state laws concerning bees to exist in your district, so check with your community, state/region, and country for laws relating to beekeeping before you start your beekeeping project.

5. Start putting your hive together by placing concrete blocks or another strong base for the hive to sit on. The hive should be sited off the ground to prevent the wood of the hive from getting rotten and to prevent another insert from entering the hive. Also, put the bottom board on the base and then, place one of the boxes on the bottom board. Lastly, put the frames in the box.

Make sure you set up the concrete blocks so they're not completely level. When you have them slightly off of the level, it will enable water to roll off the hive top. Try to read and follow the directions that came with the starter kit. The bottom board should stick out farther to create an opening for the bees to enter and exit their hive.

PLACING YOUR HIVES IN THE OPTIMAL LOCATION

1. Make sure you expose the hive to the morning sun. Place the hive in a spot that receives morning sun. This will enable the little creatures to leave the hive early in the morning to forage for pollen and nectar. Therefore, position your hive in an area that gets full sun especially if you reside in a place with cooler climates like the north-eastern United States. But if you live in an area with warmer climates, place your hive in a spot that has afternoon shade.

2. Shield the hive from direct wind. Make sure you keep the hive away from open areas that are exposed to breezes or direct wind. You can place

your hive next to windbreaks like fences, bushes, trees, or shrubbery. This will help to guaranty the health and vitality of the bees and reduce the risk of the hive falling over. Let the entrances of the hive face south or southeast if you are living in Canada or the northern United States to shield it from winter winds.

3. Try spacing out the hives about one body width apart. This is to enable you to walk between the hives without grazing yourself. When you space out the hives comfortably apart, you will be able to move freely while working and it will reduce the risk of bees perceiving your presence as a threat.

4. Don't allow the hive entrances to face foot traffic. Position the hive entrance in such a way that it is facing away from people and animals that are likely to walk past it. This will reduce the danger that the little critters will perceive people and animals that walk past the hive as a potential threat.

PLACING THE BEES IN THE HIVE

1. Find a good source for the purchase of your bees. The easiest way to purchase bees is to visit a local, well-respected beekeeper, gardening or pet stores and buy bees from them. You can also find out from the source you are purchasing your bees about where they obtain their bees to ensure you're getting quality bees. There are some sellers of bees on the internet but you won't be able to inspect the bees prior to purchase, and there's the possibility of receiving a weak hive.

2. Think about the type of bees you want before you buy. There are four main kinds of honey bees which include hybrids, Carniolans, Caucasians, and

Italians. Italian honey bees are typically the most popular bees people keep due to the amount of honey produced by them. Although Caucasian bees are known to be the gentlest of the honey bees, Carniolans are known to be strong bees that can withstand the winter very well and a variety of the hybrid honey bees have be created by beekeepers to take the traits of the other bee varieties.

3. Source your bees early in the year; around January or February. It is best to buy bees in the spring when there is plenty of food around the new colony. So, set up your hive and start keeping bees. Make sure you contact different suppliers to ensure backup bees if there is any disappointment from your chosen supplier. Having a source for bees,

guarantee that you can introduce your bees to the hive when plants start to bloom. A swarm of bees can also be caught in the wild and introduced to your hive. Some bees have outgrown their previous hive and are searching for a new home. Typically, you can only catch swarms of bees in the spring and it requires some patience and skills to populate a hive in this manner.

4. Place the queen in the hive. Your bees will come in a package that includes a queen bee and thousands of workers. So, when starting a new colony, you need to put the queen bee in the hive in the container that came with her. Generally, the queen bee will arrive in a small package with a small cover that can be removed. When you open

the cover, you'll still find a layer of candy that is used to block her. The worker bees will leave their container, fly up to the queen and chew away the candy plug to release her within some days; this will enable the worker bees and the queen to become accustomed to one another. However, make sure you follow the instructions you find on the packaging the bees arrived in.

5. Shake the workers into the hive. Once you are done with the queen bee, the next thing to do is to introduce the bees into the hive. Tap the container gently to loosen the cluster of them. Then carefully open the cover and pour the little critters into the hive. Once you have done this, you will find some of them left in the container that came with them;

simply place the open container just outside the hive and the remaining bees will find their way in. When you have the majority of the bees in their hive between the frames, place the inner and outer cover on the hive.

To make this easier, try to feed the bees well before unpacking them so they will be quiet and gentle (prepare a syrup by mixing 1 part water and 2 parts sugar and spread the mixture generously on the wire screen). You can also set up the colony in the late evening to minimize the possibility of some of the exploring worker bees getting lost. As it gets darker, they will not go too far and will return to the hive naturally. And in the morning, the bees will hover for a while near the entrance of the hive to get their bearings from the appearance of their home base and surrounding landmarks before they leave to forage. Once they have done this, they will never forget their hive except you transfer them to a new place.

TENDING TO YOUR BEES

1. Make sure you protect your bees from other creatures that like honey with barriers. Shielding the bees from predators will guarantee the safety of your bees, the vitality of your colony and a fruitful harvest. You may apply the instructions below to keep invaders away:

- Lift up the hives to keep out skunks and opossums from the hives.

- Set up chicken-wire fences or electric barriers to keep skunks, opossums, and bears at bay

- Keep bird feeders away from the hives

2. Feed your new colony until it becomes established. To give your bees a good start, you need to give them nectar made of one part water and two parts sugar. Fill a bee feeder with the sugar syrup and turn the perforated can upside down over the opening that's on the hive's board. Then, let the bees be for the next 4 days or so to enable them to get down to business undisturbed but you may refill the feeder when empty. After four days, you may take out the empty shipping cage and remove the bottom super to lower the brood chamber to the right position. And now you have a growing colony of bees.

When your colony becomes more established, you won't need to feed it much sugar syrup in the spring. However, it is advisable to always feed your bees in the fall so they can have sufficient food supply to get ready for winter.

3. Monitor and inspect your hive at regular intervals. When your colony is in place, make sure you keep an eye on their health to ensure the colony is flourishing; building healthy combs and does not have any pest or any other issue. To scrutinize the inside of the hive, you need to smoke the bees to get them submissive. When they become docile, you can start taking out each of the frames inside the hive to inspect them. During the inspection, make sure the honeycombs are forming correctly and that they aren't any other types of insects in the hive. Also check for potential issues like:

- Deformed wings

- Lack of larvae

- Visible hive beetles or wax moths on the comb

- Weakened colony

- Misplaced bars

The amounts of time that is required to tend to the hives change seasonally. Nurturing bees is a seasonal work and this means you do more work in the summer and spring. And you need to inspect the hive at least once a week during the bee's active months. Beekeeping requires very small work at the end of fall and all through winter when you simply need to inspect them once a month.

4. Make more space available to the bees as your colony develops. Honey bees typically make use of the frames provided to procreate and to store honey. Therefore, as the colony grows, there is the need to include more frames to support the growth of the colony. When the existing frames are nearly filled, you need to place another box on top of the old box. Usually, the new box that is filled with frames is used for storing honey, while the older box below helps with reproduction.

5. Collect honey once the colony gets established. The good thing is that you can harvest some honey

for yourself once the colony is strong. However, be sure that the colony is really flourishing before you take their honey. It is good if you can wait until the end of a colony's second summer before taking honey. You can easily harvest honey by removing the frames that are full of honey and cutting off the wax that caps them off. When the combs are opened, you then drain the honey out of them with an extractor the or by placing the combs in a container to drain for some days. You can turn the wax capping into candles and other items.

CHAPTER FOUR: ABOUT BEEKEEPING

BEEKEEPING EQUIPMENT

Once your bees are completely settled and getting into production, you will surely need to inspect them regularly as well as removing surplus honey for your own use. These jobs will be much easier for you if you're armed with the right equipment, which is quite affordable and worth buying and you can also make your own too.

1. Hive: The hive is the first equipment you need to acquire even before sourcing for bees. This bee equipment is very essential because it is a natural and beautiful space you can use to house your bees. Modern hives with movable frames enable you to have an easy honey removal and bee's inspection. The interior measurements of a hive and its components are very accurate. They are designed based on the "bee space" (about 5/16-inch deep or wide). The correct spacing is vital because if spaces are too small, the little creatures create brace combs and join the frames together. In a modern hive, you find a hive stand, bottom board, brood chamber, a queen excluder, supers (chambers above the brood chamber), frames, and inner and top covers.

2. Bee jacket with veil: A bee jacket with veil is very essential since bees tend to attack mammalian intruders. When you wear the mysterious-looking head coverings, you will simply feel like a kid again and you can approach the hive with confidence to perform any task you want to do and get it done thoroughly and effectively. This safety measure is especially critical if you have a beard. Those little critters become upset when they get caught in hair and they may likely sting in retaliation. Bees also get irritated when you breathe over their backs.

3. Smoker: Another essential equipment you need as you approach your colony is a potent bee-queller. Commonly known as a smoker, this indispensable weapon is inexpensive to buy and appears as if it worth three times its price. When you want to use the smoker, tear strips of burlap, wood chips or other cloth and light them with a match. Drop the burning items into the smoker's zinc tub and compress the bellows a number of times to fire up the fuel and get it to smoke. Avoid overheating the garget and don't allow the flame to shoot out of the nozzle to avoid burning the bees. When this device start working, puff some smoke into the bottom entrance of the hive to chase the guard bees back into the hive. This procedure will cause a panic among the bees, making them think that natural disaster is taking place. They get gorge together on honey and also get ready to flee to a new nesting place if necessary. When they are in this condition, they become docile and will never sting except they get aggravated by crass carelessness. Then, raise the metal cover of the hive a bit and puff some more smoke inside the hive to calm the ones you missed the first time. Now you can take out the cover completely and set the smoker on the ground within reach just in case you need to use it again. And when you are working, it is smart to always stand to the side of the hive out of the bee guards' line of vision since they get annoyed if you stand directly in front of them.

4. Gloves: With a smoker and veil, you can certainly take care of the largest colony of bees with impunity. However, as a novice, you may want to purchase bee gloves, made of coated drill cloth or leather as a safeguard. Some gloves reach up to the elbows and some are just above the wrist; over time, you will be able to work without wearing them.

5. Hive tool: You will want to acquire a hive tool or a screwdriver to loosen the frames and supers that the bees have glued tightly since the last time you worked there. These tools have different weight grades depending on dealers but they are all the same; therefore purchase the cheapest you come across.

6. Bee brush: This tool is more useful than you can imagine, this brush is used to tenderly shift the bees off the comb or other spots you don't want the little creatures to be. This tool is also handy for repairing broken comb, harvesting honey and even for collecting a swarm. However, use the brush in moderation because these insects hate it and you'll see them stinging it nastily.

SPRING FEEDING YOUR BEES

When you have gotten your colony settled in its new home around the middle of April, which is considered a lean period for honey bees in most places since there are little nectar and pollen to gather. For your colony to develop its strength rapidly, you need to continue feeding the bees artificially for the first few weeks of their arrival. This will help to fuel early laying of eggs.

The easiest method you can use to nourish the bees is to feed them with syrup using a bee feeder. The bee feeder is just a wooden insert for the entrance of the hive. This tool is punctured with flow channel to convey sugar syrup to the hive's interior. When you turn the block upside down, you'll find a cap from a Mason jar that has been punctured to allow the contents to trickle out. This container will be filled with warm syrup that you have prepared with equal part water and granulated sugar. Heat up the water and granulated sugar until all the crystals get dissolved. However, be careful not to scorch the syrup or it will hurt your bees. In case you're considering refined sugar not to be the best diet for your bees, just know that it really helps to get rid of starvation and is recommended by almost all professional beekeepers.

Pollen is a much better food you can provide your bees even if you are using sugar syrup. There are some beekeeping supply firms that sell pollen at an affordable price. The USDA also suggests the following supplement for spring feeding bees.

- Sugar/water: Dissolve 2 parts sugar in 1 part water by weight

- Pollen/soy: Combine 3 parts soybean flour with 1 part fresh dry pollen by weight

Pour the mixture through a cloth and drape it over the frames in the brood chamber. And this is indeed the best way to nourish your bees for the first few weeks in spring.

You may also try out the following pollen alternative. However, keep it in mind that it is less satisfactory than the one mentioned above, it is recommended sometimes.

- dried egg yolk: 10%

- dry skim milk: 20%

- brewer's yeast: 20%

- casein: 30%

- soybean flour: 20%

It is more advisable to use the formula that contains pollen if you can. This will enable the bees to get on their feet and start laying eggs as fast as possible to enable more worker bees to be ready for the spring honey flow. When you feed your bees pollen early in the season, expect good results.

NOTE: It is very important to be aware that your bees must not be fed with pollen in the fall.

Anything other than sugar syrup or pure honey will kill them. Because these fussy little creatures do not excrete inside their hive, they can go for a whole winter without excreting any waste. Any adulterated food item will give the wintering bees diarrhea, and if the weather is too cold for them to go outside to release their waste, they will die in the hive. Another study suggests that pollen does not cause winter diarrhea but unripe honey, or that the colony may be too weak to withstand the cold leading to inability to constantly fan, which makes the bees to eat too much.

The best food for the bees in the cold months is the same honey the workers stored earlier in the year. And a typical colony requires about 30 to 45 pounds of pure honey and a bit of sugar syrup to make it through the cold months successfully. Therefore, a deep super which is filled with about forty pounds should be enough but most beekeepers suggest two super as a safer option. And you can paint the other empty chambers if needed and keep away in preparation for the next honey flow in spring.

SMOKING BEES

Smoking bees is an easy method of calming your bees when you want to check them. The smell of smoke from the smoker causes them to assume that the hive is in flames and they intuitively begin a fire drill. Rather than protecting their home, the little creatures begin to consume honey in preparation for swarming to find a new site. But once you are done with the inspection and stop the smoke, your bees will go back to their normal activity.

How to use a smoker

You can easily do this by puffing some smoke around the hive's entrance for about five to ten minutes before you open the hive. This procedure will start the fire drill and they'll possibly be filled with honey by the time you open the hive and they won't be able to sting you. When you open the hive, make sure you puff some smoke on the top of the frames as you inspect the hive.

- **Traditional smokers**: This device is a metal container with attached bellows for lighting a small fire. This is to aid the fuel to burn well and produce plenty of thick good smolder. Different items like tightly packed dry grass, cardboard, dried leaves, or an old hessian sacking can be used to generate smoke. Make sure the smoke is cool and doesn't burn your bees. The act of mastering a traditional smoker is somehow the most difficult aspect of keeping bees and requires practicing to start and keep it alight.

- **Liquid smoke**: In case you don't want to use a traditional smoker, you may try out the liquid smoke. This does not require any lighting, it isn't possible for you to get burnt and the smoke won't ever go out. All you need to do is to purchase the concentrated liquid smoke and dilute with water. This liquid smoke is created from condensed smoke produced by wood as it smolders. It's totally natural and can not cause any harm to the bees. To use it, just spray it with an ordinary garden sprayer. It is much simpler to use a liquid smoke compare to the traditional smoker even though it doesn't have the popularity that the later has.

BEE SWARMING

As a bee colony grows stronger, it can outgrow its quarters to the extent that the queen bee and a large number of workers and drones will swarm (leaving to find a new nesting site). Swarming usually occurs at the start of honey flow and it happens as a result of insufficient space or too much of heat inside the hive. When the bees are ready to swarm, they start to cluster in golden masses at the front of the hive. During this period some days of valuable foraging are lost and if they succeed in a swarming attempt, more than half of your colony will be lost. Therefore, a good beekeeper will try to hold down this impulse as best as he can. Below are some things you can do to prevent swarming:

1. A colony usually swarms as a result of too many bees trying to crowd in a hive with small size or with inadequate space. When you add a new foundation or a few empty supers of used comb, it will make the restless bees to be satisfied to stay instead of splitting the colony.

2. Swarming can also be prevented by clipping the mother's wings or confining her inside the hive by using a queen trap, a perforated metal gadget or a wire that fits the entrance of the hive and that permits just the smaller worker bees to pass through. After you have taken these precautions,

your babies may fly into the air cheerily, bustling like a low-flying plane; however, once they become aware that their queen is nowhere to be found, they will awkwardly find their way back home and forget the whole swarming thing till the following year.

3. If any swarm, however, succeeds in leaving the hive, they won't be able to go far initially. This is due to the fact that the mother is not used to the bright daylight and she finds it hard to fly for a long time; the only times she flies is during mating and swarming. Therefore, wherever the queen lands, the remaining bees will surround her. She stays there buzzing on a close by bush, rock or tree branch, waiting for the scout bees to come back with news of a new nesting place. If you are able to find part of

your bees in this state, simply get an empty super with foundation frames and carefully cut the branch they're clinging to. However, if their position will not allow you to gather them in a cluster, simply get a cup or ladle and spoon them tenderly into a cardboard box or basket. Don't worry; they will not sting you because a new swarm is satisfied and relaxed. This is true since the worker bees have prepared for the swarming by filling themselves with enough honey to create new comb in their home and it's generally known that honey-gorged bees will not sting except greatly annoyed. So don't think you can handle them roughly because if you do, they will surely retaliate.

4. After you have secured your bees on the branch

or in a box; shake some of them into a new hive, place the rest of them on a white sheet and lay it directly in front of the hive's entrance. If you're able to find the mother; once you hive her, the rest of them will follow suit. Make sure you hold her carefully by the wings or thorax and avoid touching her abdomen so as not to injure her or ruin her ability to lay eggs. But if you can't find the queen, don't worry as bees typically take the clue and will enter the hive eventually.

5. If the newly hived bees stay where you place them for a few days that means you've doubled your colonies free of charge and very fast too. The remaining workers in the first colony will instantly nurture a new queen. However, the only

disadvantage of having two separate smaller colonies is they will produce less honey compare to a single large colony. Even at this, many beekeepers believe that separating a colony in this manner is a cheap way of filling hives and they suggest doing this just before the bees will be ready to swarm.

HARVESTING HONEY

As a colony develops, the storage cells in the brood chamber get filled up in no time and you will need to add one frame at a time for you to remove surplus, honey. This stage normally takes place between mid-June and mid-July in northern states and you can share out of your babies' harvest shortly afterward. If you so desire, you may take out a frame that's filled with honey; cut out the comb into hunks and sell or enjoy it like that. If you want to do this, ensure you make use of the thinnest foundation you can purchase so you don't feel like you're eating the spine of a fish.

However, if you prefer liquid honey, you will need to acquire a honey extractor. This device is a simple centrifuge that is built in a motionless stainless steel reservoir that has a honey entry at the base. Some of these honey extractors are quite costly but if you check around, it is possible to find a beekeeper or farmer around who is ready to sell a well used garget at an affordable price. Some beekeepers even make their own extractors that function as well as store-bought versions.

CONCLUSION

Keeping bees is an interesting and amazing craft that's open to everyone, however; it takes a lot of doggedness and time to become skilled. It's continually changing with the seasons and all parts of this craft have to be considered as a part of nature's cycle in the year.

In the beginning, most time is spent on becoming more experienced and this is actually possible with practical work. Therefore, the experience is best obtained by working with a skilled beekeeper at an established apiary or a local association.

Just like all other livestock farming, experience and education is the key to giving your bees the most favorable environment and also providing yourself with the most satisfying experience.

Also by Mark B. Chase

Dog Training

A Simple Guide to Training Your Puppy: Basics, Behavior Shaping, Potty Training, Dog Tricks, Suggestions for Training Older Dogs, Solutions to Common Problems and More

Printed in Great Britain
by Amazon